white light
primitive

§

Aidan

white light primitive

§

Andrew Stubbs

HAGIOS PRESS
Box 33024 Cathedral PO
Regina, Saskatchewan   S4T 7X2
www.hagiospress.com

Copyright © 2009 Andrew Stubbs

All rights reserved. No part of this publication may be reproduced, stored in a retrieval system, or transmitted in any form or by any means without the prior written permission of the publisher or by licensed agreement with Access: The Canadian Copyright Licensing Agency. Exceptions will be made in the case of a reviewer, who may quote brief passages in a review to print in a magazine or newspaper, broadcast on radio or television, or post on the Internet.

Library and Archives Canada Cataloguing in Publication

Name, Author, 1948-
ISBN 978-0-9783440-8-5

Edited by Paul Wilson.
Designed and typeset by Donald Ward.
Cover photograph courtesy of David Clemons
Cover design by Yves Noblet.
Set in Times New Roman and Gill Sans.
Printed and bound in Canada.

The publishers gratefully acknowledge the assistance of the Saskatchewan Arts Board, The Canada Council for the Arts, and the Cultural Industries Development Fund (Saskatchewan Department of Culture, Youth & Recreation) in the production of this book.

for Helen, Dan

§

contents

introduction
 The end of the war ... 9

war
 war ... 14

interiors
 my father's lives ... 24
 postcards ... 25
 flying dreams ... 26
 interiors ... 27
 for my father on his 75th birthday ... 29
 freud ... 30

white light primitive
 estevan saskatchewan ... 32
 white light primitive ... 36
 the mountains of saskatchewan ... 37
 conversation, south saskatchewan ... 38
 prairie light ... 41
 another harmony ... 42
 virtual reality ... 43

funeral music
 homecoming ... 48
 sunday among others ... 50
 faith, saskatchewan ... 51
 globalization ... 53
 unbreakable ... 54
 spy story ... 56
 fire and ice ... 57

cities
    carpe diem at blue hotel ... 60
    paraplegic's flying dreams ... 61
    games ... 62
    office affair ... 63
    nudes climbing apple tree ... 64
    poolside ... 65
    hearing death talking ... 66
    janet and terry ... 67

rising for air
    dedalus ... 70
    colouring ... 73
    helen, now ... 74
    weather ... 76

the disappearing art
    bad in bed, same with your poems ... 78
    flight ... 80
    houses, regina street ... 81
    the disappearing art ... 84
    alzheimer's ... 86
    ferris wheels ... 87
    house is an inlet ... 89
    victim ... 90
    rising for air ... 91
    philosopher in love ... 92
    quantum ... 93
    sunday gets into your head ... 94

acknowledgements ... 95

introduction

the end of the war

§

My father kept a shoebox of pictures he took during the war – his war – on the floor of his closet.

I'd slip into his room and go through these now and then, curious. They showed the Europe he crossed (England, France, Belgium, Germany) in the years he was overseas, 1944-45. I don't think I knew what I was looking at. It was a hodgepodge. Shells of buildings, bodies, men in uniform playing baseball on the beach.

The pictures weren't, as I say, organized, weren't in an album like the ones my mother took. So they were part of memory but not official (if that's the word) memory. Official memory was me, my brother, sisters, standing at attention, blank smiles on our scrubbed faces. It was a big deal getting your picture taken (we were told, *today you're getting your picture taken*). It was an occasion: you held your breath so as not to fidget, spoil the shot. The need to do things right first time was impressed on me at an early age. I hated getting my picture taken (the camera saw me strangely). But my mother felt a natural duty to record and preserve. Her idea of immortality was the photographic equivalent of staying in the lines when colouring. She hated the passage of time as much as I came to – blurred vision meant something was dead.

As I went through my father's pictures I learned a lesson. You can look straight at a thing and not see it, despite the cool, apparently natural co-operation of picture and reality. I was intrigued by corpses. Male genitalia, women's breasts, but the bodies looked like they were showing off. Like they were just playing dead.

Some time in the spring of 1945 my father's RCAF unit packed their trucks and drove to Belsen. My father was second driver on one of the trucks, which meant he took the wheel if the driver got shot (there were snipers in the woods). In the pictures my father stands at the double barbed-wire fence. He's handing chocolates, cigarettes to stick people in striped uniforms. Someone pointed at his camera, an ordinary box brownie such as everybody had in the fifties. It came back pregnant with stomach-churning scenes of horror. The camera saw what my father didn't see, not literally. He developed the film when he got back to base on high-contrast air force film. The clarity astounded me, obscuring sight. I didn't see war, carnage, death, just Rorschach smears of shadow and light.

My father volunteered to enlist rather than wait to get conscripted because he wanted to be in the air force, not the army. The air force, "the gentleman's service," appealed to his sense of what was proper. Also, he could learn a trade, so it was practical (assuming he'd be back). The morning he joined he was told to go home, tell family and friends goodbye. That night he reported to Union Station in Toronto and was soon on his way to Brandon, Manitoba. Then Dafoe Saskatchewan. In Dafoe he learned photography, and how to survive prairie winters. Coincidentally, *his* father had emigrated to Saskatchewan from Nottingham. My grandfather earned his way across the Atlantic scrubbing below-decks on a cattle boat. He'd been romanced by the Canadian government's promise of land – work the farm for three years and it was yours. But he got frostbite in the ear and left before his time was up. He headed east, got married, had two sons.

It was my father who got to go overseas, retrace family roots, which were of course under siege. His parents didn't expect him back, so they gave his things away – assorted *Doc Savage* and other pulps, clothes, his dog. My father's childhood thus struck me as a mystery. Unless, of course, the war was his childhood. Whereas my mother's early years were fully documented – and not just in pictures. She could recall the exact day, even the time of day anything happened – people moving, kids getting in trouble, a visit from a relative. She could tell you what was said, what people were wearing, what the weather was. Her mother was blind from a young age, so (the story goes) she took in details for two.

Around our house were lamps, ashtrays, other utensils my father made out of parts of fuses supplied by my mother. While my father was overseas, my mother did war work at GECO, a munitions factory in Toronto's east end. The fuses became souvenirs. They were arranged neatly on shelves my father built in the basement. We weren't allowed to touch, i.e., *play* with them, in case they got broken. There are pictures of my mother in the *GECO Newsletter* in her white uniform. She's leaning back against a table, eyes laughing, staring into the blue skies of future peace and prosperity. A Hollywood pose – I thought of her as someone who could have won a beauty contest or been a movie star. *If it hadn't been for the war and the sacrifices. . . .* Once in a while a famous Hollywood personality would drop in and tour the place, like Zazu Pitts. Workers were told how important their work was. Each night my mother went home, checked the death columns in the *Toronto Star*.

While in training, my father got paid extra to put in flying time (this was the air force, after all). He'd swing into a Harvard, ride out over the Quill Lakes, snapping cloud formations. He said he tried to find a different shape every time (a union of functionality and art). When a west coast invasion seemed imminent, he was sent to Pat Bay on Vancouver Island. When the invasion didn't happen, he shipped east, departing Halifax New Year's Eve, 1943. He arrived in Liverpool four days later. Some time before, on one of his trips between coasts, he got married. His passport to go on the continent after D-Day is stamped June 6, 1944. He strolled up Juno Beach one week after the landings (I note this was before the Falaise Gap was secured. It wasn't a sure thing the Allied beachhead was established). He recalled the nonchalance of French villagers – he said he didn't think they were treated that badly by the Germans, this far from Paris, *or maybe one bunch of foreign troops looks the same as any other.*

It's not that my parents' war supplied the text of my growing up years – or it's that, but not only that. By the age of ten I'd developed a sense of empty panic, a proud solitude – what soldiers felt, maybe (but I'd never been in a war). The dead, too, felt nothing, and, I supposed, the living forget. Peace wasn't just chaotic and brutal but dull, now and then humiliating, and I figured war was like that. I took it as a sign of our willing, guileless complicity in our fate. Peace, like war, is the triumph of routine, an ongoing feeling of denouement. Then there's the need for separation: war, like peace, is a community of strangers.

My parents lived apart for three years after they were married and words kept them in touch across an ocean. Words cemented them in the strangeness of their lives after my father's return, after "total victory" had been achieved. My father stood in the wreckage of his time, not knowing what to say. Like my father, I didn't really know what war was. But pictures have a way of settling in the memory, become a rain-stained window on the life you think you're living. War is a maze that lets you see what isn't war, or a time beyond war, or not yet war. So, I guess, we see sadly, though (illogically) always with the hope of safe return.

war

§

One man – one war – that's all he's usually good for.
>	Milton Acorn
>	*The Second World War*

Another war without glory, and another peace without quiet.
>	Ezra Pound
>	*Canto XXI*

war

1.

three, maybe
four feet of water in here,
clothes bedding
everything
afloat. we had to
bail the tent
out before we ate, shaved.

death squads can't bury
the bodies fast enough
smell hangs
in the air as
we keep on
going. it's where we

are, the roads,
farms where something's wrong, something
you thought you
fixed is still broken.

we're told at all times
what to do. this comes
somewhat as a surprise. it
makes sense.

pick out shapes very far
away, a house a
church still standing, say it, the name,
try out your
french
every so often.

2.

but thanks for the
cigarettes, chocolates.
I've forgotten what my
face looks like.

came to the wall of what was once a school house, a window
with dark, black
almost, sky all around,
some trucks, no road, forest
with lots
of white cavities (you'd say their
teeth are bad ha ha)
between thin, pointed tree
trunks. the trees are
white, shining, a hundred yards away.

the more we are on the move
the deader I get inside. crawled
under a truck when the air raid went off,
unthinking. it took me

seconds to realize,
can't say I was lucky. when
it comes it'll
make sense of every
thing. it might not
come. well, it'll
come, not here,
maybe not for years.

white light primitive

I like to know if a place we come to has
voices. when it's quiet they talk in
a clicking whisper like somebody choking.
they change. some have
been dead a long time. I call to them if I wake up
in the middle of the
night, which isn't a
good time. better during daylight.

3.

we move in
trucks, units of three. one
to clean up, anything
left. one in the
advance. a machine
gun going off last night woke the camp,
some MPs down the
road. it was the CO
demonstrating
what gunfire sounded like
for the
canadians.

4.

I don't think
of what'll happen. it's part of being locked in
to what is. just what is.

four days to come across. we docked in
liverpool. we came in
the *ss louis pasteur*, which was used in
the mediterranean for
cruises. on the last day we went

to action stations, firing
the guns, cleaning them out.
they had to wash the
decks
with everybody sick.
at first we thought they'd spotted a
u-boat we talked
about the whole trip.

time goes by, reminds me of
peace.

war, sudden death, remind
me of peace.

london, coming out of the beaver club,
night, up the mall to the hotel
we're staying while in
training. siren going
off, not knowing what to do just pressed against
walls huddling, watching the shrapnel
fall. one piece in the middle of the
road, lying there, white hot,
hot as sun stroke. one of the
boys running over to pick it up, keep it for
a souvenir. swinging
his arm in the air
cursing jumping up and
down.

white light primitive

5.

crossed at rheine, in
to germany. enemy country (the signs say). I got a
shot out the back of the truck. we're moving so every
thing's blurred. first thing
we come to is a
warehouse bowls plates house
hold items we use to shave.
spend the night,
morning in germany. waking up to
the cold air, engines starting, familiar
noises.

6.

new year's day 1945, fire
dropping in our backyard my
first close-ups, day and night, never
stopping. watching for paratroops anything everything
that moved in the sky in the distance. can't
remember if the pictures are true, guts
of a spitfire a field burning. we think
of machines as alive feel sorry for them.

going through my pockets these
pictures I've been carrying place to place of
you, the places you've been
but don't know, never
got to see. we go up the
tree lined road to
the death camp
where people stand
at the fences, reminded of all silent
waiting, being patient, for

the right time. right times and wrong times,
time to eat and time to work. we take up a
collection, cigarettes, pass this
across the double wire. someone motions
to give him my camera. the camera comes back, shows the holes

open, cement tables, ovens with black
stains, guard towers. it's a tuesday if I
remember. and somebody, one of our dispatch
riders, up too far, is
hit in the helmet. it misses his skull by fractions of
an inch. he shows us the hole, one of those
gung ho types. but he stays a
lot closer to the convoy on the way back.

7.

northern germany luneberg hamburg
lubeck as it's ending. we sit in
rows. may / june 1945.
the war gets away from
us again. we
go home or sign up to
fight the japs. the
circus is coming. they're setting up high wires,
trapezes. we play baseball on

the beach, paint a red maple leaf on a
launch we commandeer. cruise on the
rhine, hours
being young again, toronto canada running
home for supper late, yelled at by a cop
for spitting on the sidewalk.
seeing german soldiers loaded
on the trucks. the

white light primitive

truck pulls ahead, stops. they fall.
then more
are piled on and we think of this as
amusing. it's funny they can't
be killed any more.
war is in our bodies. we see
with war, all dead
things becoming gentle,
restful. the living are the
smell. rubble. hunger.
without death there
wouldn't be anything to talk
about. memories to make us powerful, empty.

epilogue: homecoming, september 1945

doesn't feel like I've really been.
had to hand in a luger I
was keeping for a
souvenir. if they find it you
lose your turn on the boat.
today I think I'm in the
picture and you are smiling.
strange pulling it
out, seeing you've never
changed your expression once,
like a hope
that's kept me
alive. I'm still
afraid. the speeches and movies have just
begun. I think I see it, the whole thing, once,
then it's gone.

coliseum, CNE, september 1945. you
watch for me but don't
see me. we all
look so much
alike, waves of
men marching in the darkness. go
back to everything we were
before, our hunger,
being alone.
finally touch through the crowd.
tell myself this is it, glancing
between the noise, cries,
other lives. what feels at
this moment like
war. the living are
our grave now.

white light primitive

interiors

§

"That is my face," said Rhoda, "in the looking-glass behind Susan's shoulder – that face is my face. But I will duck behind her to hide it, for I am not here. I have no face. Other people have faces; Susan and Jinny have faces; they are here. Their world is the real world. The things they lift are heavy. They say Yes, they say No; whereas I shift and change and am seen through in a second.

Virgina Woolf
The Waves

my father's lives: a portrait in three elements

father going for walks beside
the river
            becomes
the river.

he was never the
ground. that always got
away, running back to
its depths. he didn't
think dirt could keep
secrets, not from him.
under this earth more earth,
always more of the same.
hands could take
engines apart, knock down walls, plant
fence posts. *a day's work a day's pay* he said
puts food on the table.

light was his cause. solid. a thing
not spreading and
diffuse but an act,
decisive, like his saws, hammer.
it came and went. he
liked knowing where it was at all
times so he could snap
closeups of surfaces it landed on. then he'd face it,
rimming ordinary objects
with fire, trees telephone wires with
that purifying haze exploding from
them like consciousness.

then it left, without ever letting
him know what was
                  safe, what wasn't,
to look at.

postcards

my father loved my mother enough
to marry her leave for war
in the fall of 1942. in the pictures
she's shy in her
                          bathing suit, walking away, sky
unfurling like a sail. *war*
never ended
he tells me *you*
forget you're in a
war
remember,
flat tits of
the women, men their cocks
dry and
small in death.

flying dreams

father always saying he wanted
to die in paris
though he'd only been
once. that
was in the war. I think I know
why he didn't go
back, memory tricks you. he
liked having solid ground under

him. like the
country he married, a
smaller braille
of sky and mud he
ploughed to keep us fed.
winter our season,
nights his terror came
to me, sound of
his breath, quiet deaths

in dreams he taught me
to kill. I have
boxes of photographs, skins of
burned out cities (he isn't in many of them) think of
children he could've
had women he might have
taken, terrible silences, saved for
me.

interiors

father built a fence to
keep the back
yard in, took three
years
      working sundays
section by section
every summer. every winter we
climbed it, belly flops in
the snow banks over
my head. it got so high it
blocked the view into the
neighbours' yard. mother made him take it down.

he used the wood to
make shelves down
the basement for her
canned
      vegetables. we tried to plant a
garden once. the weeds were bad she hated
snakes,
one time came across
                  a frog that
scunnered her. ants got
into the leaf lettuce
so it had to be thrown
out.

he built a table
for my new
electric train with
mountains, tunnel, a bridge, buildings
                              made of milk cartons painted
gray, like the office he worked. you
could see for miles, every angle, and the
only thing that moved
was the train along
complicated
inner roads towards the station where
people always waited.

for my father on his 75th birthday

father your old body shakes
to hold a fork it
is white stone lying on
the creek bed
squirting fountains
between your teeth. your
calm is perfect, is
round like a fruit bowl. it
holds an ocean you crossed
twice thirsting after childhood.
inside I wonder
if you still think of the sound
of car engines revving in the
driveway kitchen walls shaking
windows slammed shut
to drown noise. smell of oil,
rust on your hands, in front of me,
clicking away, pictures
of streets, skating
rinks, a fence we
climbed looking for
baseballs.

freud

> To refrain from imitation is the best revenge.
>
> Marcus Aurelius
Meditations

they were small rooms built for
secrets. the age let
us vivisect. we
named valleys. extremities. drained metaphors.

which called up dreams:
open coffin, father awake
in the son's dream, son
dead, father comatose. candle
falling on the sheet and setting it on
fire. after the funeral the nails
of white light we

saw cell, nerve, the blue
circuits lighting the species' history:
what my father told me
what his father told him.

white light
primitive

§

love is form, and cannot be without
important substance

> Charles Olson
> *The Maximus Poems*

estevan, saskatchewan

1.

on our side of the
street the sidewalk was
cracked like my knee
where I fell. a man
helped me up, gently
took my hand. I
couldn't get the smell of
his aftershave out of
my dreams. at
night I could
hear bees
massing,
semis grinding gears.
I got scared. I'm
still scared. but every day I
tell my daughters: we
are here for the
duration.

2.

elevator stops between floors. I
climb onto the roof but
it starts up again. I
hear the talk as
they get on and off. space
contracts as we
            reach the top. I'm afraid.
people are saying

*neutron stars, believe it
or not, half the size of
walmart. in black holes gravity's
off the scale, like the head
aches I get after a
margarita*

I light a candle, accidentally
set fire to hundreds of dead
flies, a grave
yard in flames. people in
the elevator look up. the building will be
evacuated. accountants first, programmers, senior
        administrators last. they've been instructed
to leave papers, books behind.

3.

there's been a murder, a needle through some
thing's eye. which is a
metaphor therefore harmless
though you're filled with resentment
for life. I remember when I got
slivers walking barefoot on logs in mother's garden.
growing
up I thought I'd finally
learn to dart silently from
cloud to cloud like a soul
like amelia earhart. seeing pictures
of me as
a child: I can't remember
who drew the
barbed wire around my eyes, though it brings
distance close again.

white light primitive

4.

as space around me grows
tight I lose weight. I'm
not the waterfall but particles
of river up
stream biding time.

thoughts spread backward. I'm here and
there. both. wires binding twin selves. on either bank
the city rises like a prayer.

maps tell us the city is
flat. but over me they've built bridges,
railways. the dead are buzzing
in my ear. car horns blast, 747s
prepare their descent.

5.

the face of the side
walk is cracked like my hands. it's a
two way journey, like the stories
I've often told you. this is a face
that's given itself away many times,
like once I blurted
out *take me with you*. the only
ones who never leave are
the nuns. they stroll in pairs, always
stare straight ahead.
they never have to cross
the road, but they can't grow old
either. I'm getting better and
better at seeing lines under
people's skin: I know what you'll look like
in five years, ten years. this is
the secret I carry. by the way I think of secrets as
blue like blue cheese, some
kinds of fish, the lips of men frozen alive.

white light primitive

land: the part of
you that sees out,
calligraphy
of fence posts. think of
exit, one lone smoke trail its fire
round. a beach ball
pumped tight. the video comes back
and you can
tell it's me. mouth set, touch
myself to
make sure it's not some
look-alike. meanwhile, the
camera senses
give and take
of extremes, as
distance vanishes inside, a
way of hanging on.
I'm watched and watched,
a thing I hold in my womb, not
talking except to repeat myself. I
say mother and
mean somebody else.

the mountains of saskatchewan

one summit between two rivers
is bad lands. fences clear at ten
miles. flat taste of
talk (the farmers say) head
north in any direction: the field at night
is white gum a sound in
each root. no more green
histories. today's crop rises to the
horizon.

conversation, south saskatchewan

1.

the map lies open the map is
not on the map. we
drive for hours, white fields
flutter in unison. arrive in
the same town,
find a drugstore, order tea. the
crowd thinned, words out
in the open, on the
cenotaph. black alphabet.

2.

in the journal you
recite water, sky. colour empty of
line as tide comes in. you yell to run
then stand perfectly still.
in the rutted faces of the living
ancestral words, catalogue
of names I could
have been.

3.

through store windows,
    we traffic in
other lives, for
example sons just back from
war. their world
touch
    ing ours, in real
time.

the living are
rumours, odysseus hearing the
sirens,
    no way he
could leave them / alone / let them be
stories, a sketchy
warning passed

father to son. he had to
              sound
the body, slip into
rapturous
nothing a feeling to
bring
    home, like money in the
bank.

4.

you remember the
rabbits, cages wide open, their last message
taped to mesh. showing up head
less, their bodies dust under
the living room rug. secret

desire for things you've given
already: missing
daughters with their wild
descriptions
of wind, hail as ceilings
bend under the strain. the

late july day is compact. it has
divided exponentially. columns of
rock with white letters. prairie rolls
over us like talk. in
the shots it's never the
same. the badlands are arranged, the

slightest movement registers.
light hangs on fence posts, you think the
real thing is there, only
inches out of reach. an itch you
can't
        scratch.

prairie light

how it takes you in, patches
      of the normal, making you
      itself.

it lasts, an ice
      blue current down from
      labrador
      washing apple green rocks. killers

from the deep. and
      in spite of the
      shock you're ready.

elements blow kisses, show cracks in
      the moon. not
      hoping for any
      deep meaning. it's

not you not your fault. just a
      wave washing over, which never
      gets here but you call

to the others to run.
      world sends us scripts to
      act / live out.
      as if life is

in all things, though I'm still
      afraid to call it love in
      case you're listening. boston

if
      I remember (not hollywood)
      real rain blowing
      in.

white light primitive

another harmony

go against the music, not letting it
play us, look
for us and
most times find
us.

rain in your eyes
your daughters' eyes
you and not you,
bent to that inroad,
and love too
when it just is, when it's
gone too long. routines,
what goes with what, or
not – e.g., snowstorms in

july. what breaks into the
pattern, though it's always
the rule even when the rule doesn't
apply. well, you have to
believe, feeling your

self / inside your
self, your own
touch / breath, lying here
living, as close to empty as
it gets. this is what we do
with last words. plain, just
there. the ordinary you
carry around, place to
place.

virtual reality

1. the real sky

it's not blue, not even the
        memory of blue, but it cuts
bone. be ready be cold
where your skin peels. it's
world lover, takes
your breath away.

be safe be home
        when the street lights come on. they
are sun
flowers, sky is see through, a
knot leading else
where.
to the pain of blue.

2. where is he now?

reading *the cracker
jack book for boys*, a christmas
present from my grandfather. english boys un
tomb nazi spies, lying
death still under
canvas, riding to secret *rendez
vous* in the back of
lorries. meanwhile, kitchen table
a hockey rink salt & pepper
shaker goal posts. I always knew
the exact time, the clock
in my head ticking down,
icicles melting over the door because it's january
thaw.
power off, wait in the dark, lights back on we'd
ask (just to be sure)
how long was the clock
stopped?

3. the trojan horse

now we move out / in to
enemy country, another
     interior, flashing our
weapons, the dry
tongue of terror.
             we stake out their
sleep though their dreams aren't about
us. too bad. to
exit knock once, wait.

4. architectonic

body is an open
field, attracts filth, decaying
exponentially. yes we are
earth, give nothing off no secrets just the cold
shine of the real. we put every
thing back. listen, you
let it get inside.
the fans stay
seated, silent. it's
scary how the
eyes in the mirror follow you,
see changes you
don't. an impersonation of
outside. a white lawn a quiet in
roots.

funeral music

§

homecoming

night trespasses, stars
gather, moon drifts
southeast. arranging you,
traffic sounds. each note changes things,
you too,
            the street asking if

it's real
as you embrace it, now,
in the air of
home, fire
blazing, friends dropped in
for talk. the graves
at the end of our
street – they'd rather

be overlooked (if they
had a say) not
stroked by the diffidence of the
living, even if it's
common bond
with what we take for
granted, because
we knew it,

as grown up
talk over the TV in the 50s,
WW2, its
afterbirth,
boys our mothers knew who got
                      lost.

let
go of what
you
      can't touch.
tell yourself that.
ghosts, patchwork bodies,
what you think as you dress up in
the day, one more
chance to get it
right.

sunday among others

stucco clouds, a yellow afternoon
light, one misdirected act of
kindness, the story one
tells oneself (today)
though not sure you'll get
it, being in another
place. where land falls away / habits of
recall, now and

then. the solid matter of our lives, bodies
turning to sea / wave, history in your
eyes
not sure I've paid for
it: a chance I
mean to hand you
this, free gift of
weightlessness,
memory to travel with.

keep
it going till better times, your
body whole again, or not,
place / time. later –
meeting, but just the
story.

faith, saskatchewan

delete: e-chats after class,
students, their poems,
IT workshops in winnipeg
though it's summer
(finally) june rain settling
into prairie heat, sun hovering two
feet above socialist bald spots.
canada geese shit freely, being
       symbols, though they still stop traffic. even

raw nature has no
life. it just is, like
stale candy canes
that turn up one day in your sock
drawer.

yes I wanted you, in my bed. a letter,
phone calls timed to the
hour, knowing we'd be
quiet, the speed of
sound making punctuation, pauses
on the line. it got here –
adrenalin rush, your voice
musical
       across half a planet. what I said

was: size counts. the planet
is small. *if*
this were jupiter. . . . time does root
and you'd be back, all curve as they
say about the lines of

white light primitive   51

wood boats. it's a
team game,
the stuff of history. the night is /
isn't yours.
tell yourself each
day is one
more added to our lives as
museums.

globalization

san diego / march '98
imprints of warships,
too much sun, another country
floating,
built not to use. your
phone voice pissed
off, sad.

falling in prairie space,
the sky two dimensional,
earth
replacing itself each second.
inhumanity everywhere, especially
in other parts of the planet. our
best small talk given free
to total strangers. so we're
travel agents

of the heart. which is why
it's wrong to think some
thing got left out. words
tell all. like maps, letters home from wars not yet
started. words aren't secret, don't
cover for any
thing. they are what was said.

unbreakable

like a poem in
your way, not
expected. pure luck.
the scary part is the story they'll
make you tell at
work tomorrow. the ordinary day

off to one side, laws of
physics failing to explain.
a quiet break
in today's weather as it
smelled blood in the space he
took up like an
overdue library book. instead
it sets up housekeeping
in the brain of the mother
wheeling her shopping to

the dodge caravan. these
things happen. once.
forget other scenes: the
suicide bomber picking
the other apt complex,
bacteria in somebody

else's river. you'd
like to have an
affair with the news
woman, she's sharp definition,
doesn't
count,

like the base
runner picked off at third. tells
you not much is known. for sure. at
this time.

next day and next day.
truth isn't a
ticket to anywhere. it
is where we dwell.

make do. consider the phantoms of
mid-morning: how
they sense a storm
arriving. crows on wires? an ache in
the chest? but alive
in us, our feel for the
eventual. what hits
us as opposed to light that never
falls to earth. not dream
but the feeling of
a dream (virginia woolf
said) the random has a
soul, felt in
beings we might /
should have become.

it saves us
(momentarily)
from disasters we make ourselves
day by day.

white light primitive

spy story

the code under skin / red
track of night /
light after a storm
just there. every form
broken,
pain and all that,
meaning the body, its history
solid as years.
but a story, a pub
crawl – you'd
like. that problem of getting from
place to place a
small version of going through
night to morning / light. it
hooked you once: the
accident
of lust. knees brush. heart rates in sync.
it's not how it is, just how it is
for now.
memory turns every summer
into the same summer. not rows of
sun burned days spaced like sheets on a
line, but kids permanently
playing on the sand, mothers in the dark say
time to go.

fire and ice

> The world is the totality of facts, not of things.
>
> Ludwig Wittgenstein
> *Tractatus: Logico-Philosophicus*

winter adding to itself. details
of the dead fill the back
yards, smell of
pine breathing, snow
in swimming pools. followed by
april melt, local
river flood. now think
back in time from
open sky, july
heat. plan on

doing
better next time. this is
what we meant by cold in
the lungs, lying
together thinking:
we're not in one
place or other but
adrift. always
slightly new to the memories we
come from.

fact: body's white crease
on the sheets, cracks in the
brick. think of sadness, of
what goes with each
season.
facts as wishes. we dazzle our
selves with rough imagining. fact: table by
a lake. sip a diet
coke. and so you
are.

cities

§

carpe diem at blue hotel

toronto

night. your city links
up, sends itself human data –
unpaid master
cards,
      name changes by various
states.

its architecture has roots
in empty ground. roads
twist back on them
selves like divers. feel free
to go any place as long as you don't
leave. traffic curves miles below street level. under
this city there's another city, its
stillborn twin. scenic elevators only take

you so far
up so far down. you
never know how much more there
is, not moving – though you
      think you are, like a boat
going against the current.

a paraplegic's flying dreams

vancouver

his children surround him,
bend over his wheelchair
behind guard rails,
hang from the tip of the
conductor's white baton.

he's rest
less for empty time, the chaos after
parade's
end. lines of marchers break up, the
precision motorcycle

riders return to give out parking tickets. the band boards
its bus. he's afraid of being looked at. TV cameras
pan the crowd. he wants to put every
thing back, tired
of motion that leaves no outer signs,

just a gray
falling through
cloud and water.
nothing, he writes, is emptier than
childhood.

white light primitive

games

new york

inside the lines you're
safe. body
stands still the heart
beats young. men
take temporary positions like
hands of a clock. no before or

after. where you stand
when it's over is
you. this is when the
pain hits home. wear it, your
flood of green, sand and dust.

souvenir of personal
empire.
use it to buy a
post game beer.
atlantis has reverted to

dream state. you are / aren't
that other life,
meeting
of ground and ground. it
knows too much about you. the
mystery only deepens.

office affair

montreal

the organization's way of
letting you take the
afternoon

off. your boss
likes to think
giving

permission's
same as being there / doing it.
he / she is some

thing that wants to be
alive. watch for the sound of
anything mechanical. bedsprings,

the way her voice
keeps going yes more yes
more. don't think

of yourself as
good. anybody
listening (which he / she is) might

get the idea you're
irreplaceable and fire you.
don't think open

space'll catch you every
time. real men fall
when they jump.

nudes climbing apple tree

guelph

cowpokes are singing to
the school marms. it's friday night
in guelph ON.
where the songs
don't skip a beat, sweet

as liberace, as
you read the room, pick the gun
slingers
sidekicks, got all the
time
in the world, eye
balls
AWOL up there on stage.
the bobs too thin too
fat, but they itch to hand her roses when she steps
down *cuz take*
away the beat the
footlights she's still a
beaut. meanwhile the announcer's
voice is every
where in every

ear *god bless 'em all, every mummy a*
crowd pleaser and never quits, the
bobs go home or duck to
the can. they
get back, everything's changed, everything's the same.

poolside

waterloo, ontario

the moms a few dads
make faces at their kids
swing them on open knees
like
        gravity. these are risky
times. even the pale sky's
hiding, touching ground
in patches, oblongs of
gold light that knuckle the
pool's edge. but the kids get to be
themselves.
            meanwhile the afternoon breeze has
become abstract, careless. from
nowhere
the free swimming hour
ends

hearing death talking

louvre, paris, summer 1981

see through the
pictures that separate you /
us. this was once
your wish, to
be pointed at
earth's centre, where gravity floats
                                              free:
no buried life no omelet
of skin to
scare / trick you. it's all here /
now. when you die you die, not like
images, here one second gone the
                                         next. it's more like
song: slower beat
longer pauses,
until you're bored,
turn away. we think of
you and
don't change repeat don't change.

janet and terry

windsor / detroit

when he left when it
was for
sure done I handed him a twenty,
40-ouncer, he said if
I came around we could split. I went around. we humped
on his borrowed mattress, one
faded sheet.
I did a laundry right after. he
cracked the bacardi and
we watched the washing
machine go through
its cycles two
cats from
upstairs rubbing necks against
the back of our legs, in
unison.

rising for air

§

dedalus

1. in the museums of the present

we're perfect swimmers, neutral, alive
to extremes only of pleasure /
pain.

bodily memory clicks
in, what the kids are
up to in their rooms,
doors closed. later
silence, more waiting.

move through each other,
getting smaller feeling
less.

2. graffiti

to think about going is
to go. think about it.
                       everything
its own past
tense. memorize their wars, politics
but don't be part of their
suffering.
you'll never arrive
if you want the
last word.
      don't think
the last word was
his.

3. danny, early morning

danny, four and a half, got
himself dressed today.
because it's saturday. because it's raining.
other days other
weathers he's helpless. he's
his childhood self, watching last
night's snow, patches of
brown grass,
holes in the earth. he
watches himself in mid-air as
hands reach for him, lift him
gently down, land
him bloody mud
faced on the door step. then back to his
war in the sky.

4. flight

danny wears his machine, without
cracks. hockey helmet
sheriff's badge empty holster. some

thing's always chasing
him. he hides in
side his mask, his
portable backdrop,
horizon. doors to other
continents.

but he's already there already
falling. hears every
conversation,

can observe punctuate change direction.
light is risky,
he practices listening to
waterfalls:
taps left running, toilets flushing.

when we get where we're going he can be
my teacher. I promise to
let my secrets out at last.

5. case history: 1952

christmas. watching everybody
eat. they've put
paper hats on pass
food around. they
can't see me. the TV's
turned down, presents back
in boxes under the tree. I liked toys
you could take apart, later took
the wheels off my
bike, handlebars, cleaned everything
inside out. trying to make it
more my own. rarer, purer, down to the
last spoke. which made
it unnecessary to
ride. this was
my first invention of dying.
I fell in love with the pity,
sultry reticence of winter, imagining
the sun going out the white moon
crashing into our backyard, huge
giant alarm clock.

colouring

helen draws the wind grape blue,
hungry for itself,
see myself age six eating
an orange by
the living room window. her

river a wire a hole where
the sun hangs. fence posts shine.
a man walks a dog
along a brick path.
she catches me looking. her

eraser cancels pencil
marks, rocks melt back into blank paper.
along the horizon lines are
solid, trees never touch.
she aims her pencil like a telescope a field

suddenly black. canada geese
scatter behind clouds. lines of hills
play hero, alternately
smooth / rough
like a shark's back.

white light primitive

helen, now

before you were, then the
day
        presence of you, catching us off
guard. you got
here before your
name. I'm not sure it
was a gift, a few
        hours' non entity. flesh and blood
but no word to call
you with. the noon

sun aloof as death,
        what one day olds
dream? maybe.
or the routine of our
        voices,
all of us in the
room.

now of course you're 21
zero time on your
        hands
just regular talk about
daily perks /
pains, which mostly
you
        take in stride. or time (speaking
of . . .)
running, my memories of

niagara pictures
dad took of us at the edge, mom
scared
we'd be caught in
      any sudden wind / voices /
sail over the side. well we were.

but learn to trust
the real to take care of you. fear,
day in day out,
through father
      to daughter to
son. of solitude, yes. of silence.

or something in the catch of our
bodies, ghosts you
registered
before you knew the
      names of the world, of
things that are. I'll

say this: any
thing's better than that slow fading
of the ordinary, our blind
will
      to forget. then trying to
say we've lived. the
white stain where the heart

should be. regular as
long distance phone calls, thoughts of
years, the hours
between us, working
      those numbers every
time we talk.

weather

sunday a.m. critical mass
undisturbed
so far on
roads lawns.
cosmic chance –
      cold came,
killed mythology (before its
time) no tire
tracks,
      nothing
to tell surface from
depth. though hours
from now it'll lose
itself in the debris of waning
day. make us think, oddly, of
      heat, bundling up in incoming
dark. ending with you in the
room. toaster, kettle boiling, love
not out of the question.

the disappearing art

§

bad in bed, same with your poems

it happens on the
prairie as nowhere
else, an uninterrupted view to
outer planets, space
your life raft.
but paranoia too, as in:

elevators stand perfectly at
attention, waiting for the martian
landing. lesson: taking
protocol seriously in childhood
can make you frigid,
bad in bed, same with your
poems.

the real gives / takes, *quid pro
quo*. not bad news if you
ingest it slowly, the way
you'd come into a small town, full of
moon, vapor trail: what do
humans add to the
real? once we'd seen it, it was.
there. no need to talk.

lesson: keep the body
empty
      of imagining, or
connection from moment to moment improvised like
the heartbeat of the common man.
this will cost
you not less than the
bundle.

or: the real won't give you
        a good poem from a
bad idea. lies
show up like bugs in
your teeth, or your first
fear of this
place: feeling the earth's orbit
underfoot.

it's the pain of
every day, years
        in the making, in the roundness
of wanting. except nothing is
conscious, just forces that
at certain times in certain
places made you say the line
of land wasn't blue

or green, or
bluegreen. not separate but
single, the moon's blackness.

flight

from up here every
lawn's an albino
with beachball eyes and a shy
smile that comes and goes like a
paycheck.

wind and sunlight ride the vertical like
jacob's angels. you've been here before,
yes. and rosenkrantz and
guildenstern are the same
geezer written twice. you

know this from
submersion
in icy air, prairie fizzing at the
horizon, sunlight serving
champagne breakfast. the

moon drove north, its circumference was every
where. rain and fire can't be
repeated. look down, it's
the same beach, the same
coke, sandwich, pink tablecloth, ferris wheel.

houses, regina street

1. voices: above ground

a house is a shore
line, night morning after
noon, sidewalks edgy in
the blond air.
tell them no / not / not to
day.

2. voices: below ground

inland houses are
valleys:
the limit of the human to suck the land
dry, stuff the river mouth with
ice.

3. voices: somnambulant

but a house is. if a house stood still she'd be
winter, snow dying early that year,
garter snakes hatched
in our rootcellar, the
grass crawl
ing.

4. voices: in season

he barefoots it to
the toilet, lights the
stove. moons for breakfast every day, every day
she tells him
you belong to the season.

5. *voices: voyeur*

his last day,
watched through the
back fence, a blue truck growing smaller.
the road was
       maroon the sunset

inland. we didn't
know. yes / knew
but saw no (how
to say it?) blip in our
       dream

6. *voices: transparent*

remote body papery thin
dried urine
smell streetshine after a
storm. black telephone wires
that singsong over
head

7. gnosis

a house is a strip
tease a house keeps
her
        distance.

you get
to see a long way it's a long way to the
country back of your eyeball. and
prairie
blows in every
crack.

sometimes
she's a river (planted) a tree (blowing)
sometimes a spaceship
        moving inland.

virgin ground
but tough as heart
muscle. and sometimes she chases her tail, moon
light under the door her
oldfashioned house you can't stay /
go.

white light primitive

the disappearing art

> There's my last duchess painted on the wall
> Looking as if she were alive.
>
> > Robert Browning
> > "My Last Duchess"

what duke didn't figure: love's what
you get. rough justice, shock
and awe.
the night her
tryptich

got first prize she
accepted in bandages,
sold right away.
lines he tried as
she slept worked slept late.
the angst took weeks
to cure. no

body got it but they
clapped: live everything save
nothing. seasons in
london, prague, new
york. cohabitation with
fame, cockroaches. plus riverside
address. warhol said her eyes
were postcards, took you

anywhere. to her it
wasn't real. she drew him
fixated, in drag, in
faces of women in childbirth.
caption: "vision equals
life." she fell hard. "I'm god's
machine
his will be done."
pain the edge,
the mystery, all secrets out.
"so what's to talk
about?" long distance / chat trailing
off, longer silences, making do,
faded into prairie flat.

alzheimer's

the top branches write their networks on
clam shell,
rock. the lake stretches, old skin.
the flick of shark fin, scary
circles, planets.
seaweed running
from her ankles. toes
leave moist dents where
memory should
be, mistaking moonlight
for ground, ground for
shadow.

ferris wheels

her

night: a black pearl
on the heart. heads on the
glistening tarmac fishbowls –
50s science fiction. you
freeze, a lonely
blip soon to
disappear. you'd trade skin for pink
scales, swim deeper. mean

time: andy, from planet
egg, reads your mind knows what you'll

say before you
say it. butterflies in the
gut as you rise / sink. double smoke stacks
blow grease, haze. gulls dot the
breakwater. scary you think and
your english teacher says so
too. don't get caught you got the time
but just talk and mean it.

him

loop loop . . . memory upstream: purple
side shingles, sunday potroast. lost in
the raspberry bushes, butterfly bodies,
gentlest pinch of wings. jarfulls
under the steps.

now: mid-april ice breakup,
wind off the lake,
you're still hungry
for what you
can't know. a hope not

to stop. what you give
away comes back.
if it
comes back it's a
weapon.

house is an inlet

think impossible think
cezanne, apples permanently poised
to
      drop.

colours were week
days. channels I switched:

      monday: silver
      tuesday: green
      wednesday: orange
      thursday: black
      friday: white
      saturday: red
      sunday: blue

counting down / telling time. heading
home when the

streetlights came on. mean
while cezanne, robotic
pommes. rorschach blemishes

everywhere –
marilyn's mole, your
friend's mother's varicose veins.

the bathroom mirror softened
me put me
back (almost). what it
saw was
surfaces: backyard
pool blinding sunlight. slipping deeper
into shark patrolled water, a desperate cuban
on the wide sea to
america.

victim

files her body under:
mouth, brain, heart,
cunt. all ways of
sinking.

yes / no. the
quantum desire / not desire.
this is safe. she
likes to stand at the back of the

crowd, dodge the paparazzi. her
last trip home: disappearing
over roof
tops,

the impossible sky
water
you can't see
across.

rising for air

the land is open the
way her
body lies, not home
except at sunset
when windows fill
with blue TV
light. then you know it's
taken another country
into itself. the summer we
played christmas carols
out the bed
room screen. almost
conjured winter's eggshell
cold, snow in the pool. in one
of the rooms of her
mind she died.
she saw the sea
open. thought surface. thought
melting.

philosopher in love

he fell in, to what is.
ding-an-sich, thought

moon, a glass river, a
mountain,
night.

time ripened into
white light, became

hunger, lacuna.
silence
a jet trail. unpublished. all those

landscapes contracted
to an

edge of cold tickling
the
brain, as he broke.

quantum: two-way trip, july 1963

silver spines
of lake, TV
antennas,
real as long as
you don't look at them. years
later, rewinding memories
over white wine
pulling out of the station.
rain
on the glass, see
myself inside, steel wheels
tapping lines of track, as
the radio played WW2 songs.

sunday gets into your head

sunday doesn't change,
though she does wind down, two
o'clock four o'clock,
often tired
by supper. sunday
likes being seen on
the veranda sipping sangria. the
scene: carpe
diem to friends passing by.
sunday has broken
promises (usually
work for week
days) but sunday feasts you
with pink
light into the late sky
of august. no, sunday
isn't fairy tale isn't whore, just
one more day (among
others)
that falls to earth.

acknowledgements

§

Some of these poems have appeared, in slightly different form, in *The Antigonish Review*, *Carousel*, *Event – The Douglas College Review*, *The Fiddlehead*, *filling Station*, *Grain*, *The Malahat Review*, *The New Quarterly*, *Paradise Frost: The Thunder Bay Poetry Renaissance*, *Prairie Fire*, *Rampike*, and *Textual Studies in Canada*.

Andrew Stubbs teaches composition and rhetoric at the University of Regina. His interests include all phases of expository and academic writing, including management communication and technical writing, which he has taught at the University of Regina, Wilfrid Laurier University, and the University of Guelph. He is currently Co-ordinator of Writing Services for the University of Regina Student Development Centre.

Stubbs was the editor of *Rhetoric, Uncertainty, and the University as Text* (2007), a collection of articles on writing and writing theory, and co-editor of *The Other Harmony: The Collected Poetry of Eli Mandel* (2000), both published by the Canadian Plains Research Centre. An earlier work on Mandel's poetics, *Myth, Origins, Magic,* appeared in 1993. He has published articles and reviews on literature, literary theory, psychoanalysis, and creative writing. *White Light Primitive* is his first collection of poetry.